—Volum

—Hawaiian Ukulele Solos—

edited and arranged by

Gary Stewart

SE001

Copyright © 2019 by Gary Stewart
WV, USA
All Rights Reserved

ISBN-10: 1074048075
ISBN-13: 978-1074048075
BISAC: Music / Musical Instruments / Ukulele

No part of this publication may be reproduced in whole or in part, stored in a retrieval system, nor transmitted in any form by any means, electronic or mechanical including, but not limited to, photocopying, audio or visual recording, or by any means yet to be discovered, without express permission in writing from the publisher.

Published in the United States, June 2019.

Cover Art: Cover page of "I can hear the Ukuleles Calling Me," Jerome H. Remick & Co., New York, 1916. Cover edited by Vanessa Barnes.

PREFACE

In presenting these works to the public, it is my sincere hope that these books will help to fill the gap of Hawaiian solo ukulele repertoire that is currently available in print. The principal idea is to present, in various volumes, Hawaiian music of all periods and styles. Furthermore, the music within these books also contains pieces that were inspired by Hawaiian culture but may or may not have been composed by native Hawaiians, e.g., *Hapa Haole*, or *Contemporary Hawaiian songs*. These volumes will also illustrate the influence that Hawaiian music had on the world from its inception. Moreover, it will show how the little musical instrument known as the ukulele, rose to popularity, and became the apparatus that many musicians and composers alike, used, and still use, as their creative vehicle.

These books arose from my desire to have all of my Hawaiian ukulele arrangements in one place, so that when I felt in a Hawaiian state of mind, I could grab these books, and all of the music would be right at my fingertips. I hope these volumes of music will give the reader a greater appreciation of the ukulele, and inspire them to explore the history and music of Hawai'i.

Gary W. Stewart Jr.
Duffields, West Virginia
June 2019

ACKNOWLEDGMENTS

There have been many people who have assisted in the preparation of this edition, and for their interest, support, and invaluable suggestions, I would like to publicly acknowledge, and thank them. I would like to give particular thanks to Dr. Stanley Yates, of Austin Peay State University—his musicianship, encouragement, and insight have played a valuable role in shaping this edition. Dr. Charles Winfrey, and Will Perks for their sage advice, and guidance. To luthier Michael Thames, who builds the best instruments in the world. To my parents, and my brother Sean, who have always encouraged and supported me in my various endeavors. And to my former teachers, Dr. Glenn Caluda and Stephen Aron, both of whom helped to shape my playing, artistry, and musicianship. And lastly, my gratitude and love go to my beautiful wife, Yvonne, who has encouraged and supported me all the while never asking, "…is the book done yet?"

(Kolomona: Hawaiian Troubadour)
by Hubert Vos ca. 1898[1]

The *Pacific Commercial Advertiser* newspaper referred to the painting shortly after it was completed as "a strong piece of work, brimful of life and action." In the painting, Kolomona is wearing the distinctive shirt of the po'ola, or professional stevedore, who unloads cargo from ships. He also is wearing a wide- brimmed, straw hat and large handkerchief around his neck, suggesting of an occupation that requires working long hours in the sun.

---

[1] The original oil on canvas by Hubert Vos (1855-1935) is held by The Honolulu Museum of Art.

Contents

Introduction 7

    Queen Liliʻuokalani 7
    George K. Awai 8
    Ernest Kaʻai 8
    Henry Kailimai 9
    N. B. Bailey 9
    Charles E. King 10
    Hapa Haole Music 11
    Mrs. Kaukini & Ms. Martha K. Maui 11
    Thomas S. Kalama 12
    Matthew H. Kane 12
    James Fulton Kutz 12
    Sonny` Cunha 13
    Johnny Noble 13
    Jack Owens 14

Ukulele Stroke Techniques 14

The Arrangements

    Mauna Kea - Sonny Cunha, arr. by Awai 18
    Roselani - W. J. Coelho 20
    Song of Old Hawaiʻi - Johnny Noble, arr. by Kaʻai 24
    Maui Girl - Thomas S. Kalama 26
    Kuu Lini - Charles King 33
    My Dear Hawaiʻi - Charles King 36
    On the Beach at Waikiki - Henry Kailimai, arr. by Awai 39
    Sweet Brown Maid of Kaimuki - Henry Kailimai, arr. By Awai 40
    Ka Makani Kaili Aloha - Matthew H. Kane 42
    Halialaulau / Ke Aloha Poina Ole - Mrs. Kaukini & Miss Martha K. Maui 44
    Fair Hawaiʻi - James F. Kutz, arr. by N. B. Bailey 50
    Kamehameha Waltz - Charles King 52
    Paauau Waltz - Charles King 55
    Paauau Hula - Charles King 58
    The Hukilau Song - Jack Owens 62
    Pauoa Liko Lehua - Charles King 66
    Elue Mikimiki - Charles King 68
    The Hula Blues - Johnny Noble 70
    My Hononlulu Girl - Sonny Cunha, arr. by N. B. Bailey 72
    Aloha Oʻe - Queen Liliʻuokalani, arr. by Awai 74

About the Author 76

(Anthony Zablan)

Musicians like Anthony Zablan, who played at the Pan-American Exposition in Buffalo, N.Y., in 1901, helped to spark the "ukulele craze" on the mainland in the early 20th century.[2]

---

[2] Public domain photograph entitled, *Hawaiian Musician with Ukulele*. Taken during the Pan-American Exposition in Buffalo, N.Y., in 1901, by beach photo studio. The original photograph is held in the collection of the Hawai'i State Archives, call number: PP-33-4-016.

Introduction

The compositions that are contained in this book are wide and varied. They include compositions that were composed by Hawaiian Queen Lili'uokalani, to the arrangements of early 20th century ukulele players, native Hawaiian composers, and that of the Hapa Haole composers.

In his PH.D thesis *The Development of Waikiki,1900-1949:The Formative Period of an American Resort Paradise*,[3] scholar Masakazu Eiri notes that there are six forms of music which may be said to be indigenous to Hawai'i, each reflective of a historical point in time:

- Mele oli (chanting only), mele hula (chanting with hula dancing), and mele hulakui: The former two are chants related to, but not always deriving from the pre-contact era; the latter represents a chant and dance style with Western influence, developed in the late 19th and early 20th centuries from mele hula.
- Himeni: hymns related to 19th century missionaries.
- Himeni-like songs: non-religious songs related to Hawaiian royalty, based on Western melodies and harmonies.
- Hula songs: folk songs based on hula kui.
- Hapa haole songs: part-white or foreign songs, originally based on hula kui, blending with mainland popular songs. Hapa haole Hawaiian music with which most mainlanders were familiar, had very little in common with traditional island music.[4]
- *Contemporary Hawaiian* songs: influenced by Western popular music.

The ukulele is a relatively new instrument. It arrived at Hawai'i in the late 19th century via the Western world, and, as a newly developing instrument, it saw various changes in the techniques used to play it, as well as changes in musical style.

In order to better understand and appreciate the music in this book, there will be a brief analysis of the various composers' lives, musical style and the techniques they utilized.

Queen Lili'uokalani

Lydia Lili'u Loloku Walania Kamaka'eha (born September 2, 1838 – November 11, 1917) was the first ruling queen and the last sovereign monarch of the Kingdom of Hawai'i, ruling from January 29, 1891, until the overthrow of the Kingdom of Hawai'i on January 17, 1893. Lili'uokalani's early years incorporated a unique era in the Hawaiian Islands that saw a cultural merger of indigenous Hawaiian traditions with that of Western cultures after the onset of pineapple farmers and sugar plantation owners. As a member of the Hawaiian aristocracy, Lili'uokalani was exposed conversely to both circles. Her first language was Hawaiian, and she was well-versed in Hawaiian legend and poetry. However, the majority of her musical training was in Western musical forms, like hymnody and waltzes, that

---

[3] Ejiri, Masakazu. 1996. "The Development of Waikiki, 1900-1949: The Formative Period of an American Resort Paradise." Dissertation, Manoa, HI: University of Hawaii. University of Hawaii at Manoa. page, 195
[4] Alexander, Geoff. 2018. America Goes Hawaiian: The Influence of Pacific Island Culture on the Mainland. Jefferson, NC: McFarland & Co.
page 91

would shape the compositional foundation for the bulk of her musical creations. Though she is remembered in Western history as a stateswoman, her musical contributions stand in conjunction with her political career. Moreover, her compositions and poetry are renowned in the Hawaiian Islands where she endures as one of the most admired Hawaiian composers to this very day. Aloha O'e is her most famous composition and is arranged in this volume by George E. Awai.

George (Keoki) E. Awai

George E. Awai was born on December 7th, 1892 and died in 1981. Awai was well-grounded musically. Awai came from a musical family; he had started playing instruments early, first the ukulele, and then the guitar, banjo and (Hawaiian) lap steel guitar; and learned how to read music. The Panama-Pacific International Exhibition at San Francisco is what helped to spark the Hawaiian music movement of the early 20th century. It also helped to spark Awai's musical career. A competition was held in Honolulu to select the best group to perform at the exhibition. The final was between Awai's group, and that of Ernest Ka'ai. He recalls, "They picked us over Kaai's group. I was a little surprised, but thrilled, because Ka'ai's was supposed to be the best. I think he was a little mad at me for winning." Awai was only 22 years of age when his group won. The central figure in the musical promotion was George Awai who, with his outstanding Royal Hawaiian Quartet, delighted thousands of people who were hearing Hawaiian music for the first time. After the exhibition, Sherman-Clay & Company, of San Francisco, one of the largest music publishers of the day hired Awai to teach both the ukulele and lap steel guitar. Awai arranged and had published by Sherman-Clay Volume one of the "Superior Collection of Steel Guitar Solos." Included in the volume was nearly 30 selections-all Hawaiian and popular selections with some standard numbers. Also, in 1916, he co-published with N. B. Bailey "A Collection of Ukulele Solos," from which the selections bearing his name in this book were taken. This was the first ukulele tablature book of its kind. Additionally, Awai found time to compose such songs as "Sweet Lei Lehua," "Kuulei Waltz," "Hawaiian Hula," "My Ukulele Melody," and his most famous melody, "Kilima Hawaiian Waltz." When asked about trends in contemporary Hawaiian music, he said softly, "It doesn't seem to have the old sweetness of our music."[5]

Ernest Kaleihoku Ka'ai

Ernest Ka'ai was born in Honolulu, Hawai'i, in 1881, to Simon Kaloa Ka'ai, a prominent politician during the Kingdom of Hawai'i. Known as the first Hawaiian ukulele virtuoso, Ernest Ka'ai, performed all over the globe. He was unquestionably the foremost ukulele specialist of his era and had an acute comprehension of the ins and outs of ukulele playing. Ka'ai published the first ukulele instruction book in 1906. Although known for promoting the ukulele as a featured instrument in the Hawaiian orchestra, his sophisticated fingering, picking, and stroke styles also inspired the modern establishment of the ukulele as a solo instrument. In addition to his musical skills, he also owned the Ka'ai Ukulele Manufacturing Company, advertised from 1909-

---

[5] Kanahele, Edward L. 1977. "George E. Awai Fueled the Hawaiian Music Craze in 1915." Ha'ilono Mele III (9): 5–6.

1920. Although it was sold in 1917, and Ka'ai became a shareholder in the newly formed Aloha Ukulele Manufacturing Company, his namesake company apparently continued without reference to whomever was the actual instrument maker in those following years. Ka'ai left Hawaii in 1923 to tour the Far East and Australia, and eventually settled in Sri Lanka. In the mid-1930s, he planned to open a "Hawaiian Village" in Shanghai, China, but the war forced him to flee, and he returned to Hawaii in 1937. He moved to Miami, Florida, in 1941 and incorporated the Ka'ai Music Studios in 1946. He died in Miami in 1962.[6]

Henry Kailimai

Henry Kailimai (1882-1948) was born in the Kohala District on the big island of Hawai'i, the son of William Henry and Kaaipelana Kailimai (notice he took his father's last name as his first, and his mother's last name as his last; since Hawai'i was a matriarchal society, his taking his mother's maiden name is not surprising).[7] He was musician, teacher, and composer. He was a known ukulele player, but could play many different instruments, and was an accomplished singer. He moved to Oahu where he became a member of the Mormon Church and played organ for church services. He also became a protégé of Ernest Ka'ai, and worked as one of Ka'ai's musicians. Ka'ai was also his talent agent and helped guide his career. His quintet, "Royal Hawaiians," was invited to perform at the Panama-Pacific International Exposition in San Francisco (1915) and were listed as a star attraction. None other than Henry Ford, of Ford Motors, came to the exposition and was captivated by Kailimai's performance, and invited him to Detroit to become a resident musician providing music for Ford Motor Company entertainment functions. Kailimai accepted Ford's offer, moved to Detroit, and renamed the quintet the "Ford Hawaiians." The group went on to record for Edison in 1916, and from 1923 to 1925 made some of the earliest mainland radio broadcasts of Hawaiian music on Ford's Dearborn radio station. While in Detroit, Kailimai also directed the "Ernest Ka'ai's School of Hawaiian Music." Today, Kailimai is most noted for his composition "On the Beach at Waikiki."

N. B. Bailey

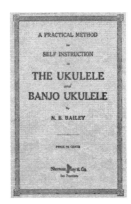

Very little is known of Bailey's life, apart from the publications that he left behind. He published several works for the ukulele through Sherman, Clay & Co. His publications include, "A Practical Method for Self-Instruction on the Ukulele and Banjo Ukulele (1914)," "Songs from Aloha Land: a collection of Hawaiian songs with Ukulele accompaniment (1916)," "The Ukulele as a Solo Instrument, C Notation: A Collection of Ukulele Solos (1916)" This publication is the source of the arrangements by Bailey which were used in this modern edition. Bailey also published a Hawaiian lap steel guitar method entitled, "The Peterson system of playing the guitar with steel in the Hawaiian manner." The ukulele arrangements and methods left behind by Bailey illustrate that he had a solid understanding of the instrument, and hopefully more information will be discovered about his life and career.

---

[6] "Ernest Kaleihoku Kaai". *The Ukulele Hall of Fame Museum. Archived from* the original *on 18 April 2012*. Retrieved 24 May 2010. The Ukulele Hall of Fame Museum.

[7] Tyler, Don. 2007. Hit Songs 1900-1955: American Popular Music of the Pre-Rock Era. 1st ed. Jefferson, NC: McFarland & Company.
Pages 421-422

Charles E. King

Charles Edward King, was born on January 29, 1874 in Honolulu to Mary Ann King and Walter Brash. He died on February 27, 1950. He was a member of the first graduating Class of 1891 of the Kamehameha School for Boys. Music was a lifelong fascination for King. He was at ease in a multicultural world, and the world of the ali'i (Hawaiian nobility). Queen Emma was his godmother, and Queen Lili'uokalani was his music teacher and a great musical inspiration. Although only a quarter Hawaiian, he was fluent in the Hawaiian language, and knowledgeable in Hawaiian culture and history. He was particularly fascinated by the mele oli, and mele hula, and knew their texts and meanings well, all of which became a source of both inspiration and material for his own compositions. He was also a keen student of the metamorphosis of chants into melodic songs. He embodied the "royal style," as it were, but he also brought it to its pinnacle through the quantity and quality of his output. But, because of his training and exposure, he actually exceeded the accomplishments of his mentors by introducing or developing more sophisticated melodies and harmonic structures, and greatly enlarging the thematic scale of his compositions. He was an innovator, but he was very much a traditionalist. These standards, which were more or less taken for granted and unarticulated until King came along, were" 1. lyrics of Hawaiian songs should be in the Hawaiian language, 2. the subject of a song should be about Hawai'i, and 3. the melodic quality should be nahenahe (sweet) and the tempo not "jazzed up." King once said: "Let us have enough pride in our own music to keep it pure." By that he presumably meant "Hawaiian." Among Hawaiian composers of his day, King was one of the best grounded in the fundamentals of music theory. Not only had he studied music from his youth, but he had also taught it in schools for many years. He displayed his technical mastery not only in his compositions—but also in his numerous arrangements, in his ability to play a variety of instruments and in his conducting of musical ensembles. He was, for example, conductor of the Royal Hawaiian Band for three years. King was a late start, however, as he did not begin composing until he was 42 years old.[8] Charles King was living proof that it's never too late to start. Rhythmically, King's songs are often in 3/4 time, perhaps more so than any of his contemporaries. However, this was quite in keeping with the style of the late 1800's. He called it his, "Hawaiian tempo." Nonetheless, his songs also include fast hula, and 2/4 march time such as "Kila Kila Haleakalā," the lively hula, and "Imua Kamehameha," the rally song for Kamehameha Schools. King's songs almost invariably call for ukulele and guitar as well. In Conclusion, it cannot be denied that the majority of King's songs are Hawaiian songs. However, he was also influenced by the current musical styles around him. For example, his song, "Honolulu Maids," composed in 1916, comes close to being "Hapa Haole," and may in fact have been influenced by Henry Kailimai's popular song "On the Beach at Waikiki" which was also composed in 1916. However, he was not dogmatic, as even though he emphasized the use of Hawaiian lyrics, the lyrics of over a dozen of his songs are in English. Preoccupation with his education and teaching responsibilities may have delayed his musical career, but it is a testimony to his character that he achieved what he did in the last half of his life.[9]

---

[8] Kanahele, George S. Hawaiian Music and Musicians: An Illustrated History. Honolulu, HI: Univ. Press of Hawaii, 1979. pages 214-217.

[9] Kanahele, George S. "Charles E. King, Consensus Dean of Hawaiian Music." Ha'ilono Mele III, no. 9 (September 01, 1977): 6-7.

Hapa Haole Music

Hula maidens in grass skirts and coconut bras, rolling surf, and little grass shacks—it's a vision familiar to those for whom the Islands are a distant fantasy, a vision often grounded on the music known as *hapa haole*. At the turn of the 19th century, as more and more mainlanders traveled to Hawai'i on new steamships, the U.S. government sponsored the Hawai'i Promotion Committee, which was put together by local merchants and leaders in the hospitality industry in 1903. This committee produced travel brochures, promotional material, and souvenir postcards. These promotional materials conjured up images that were used to promote Hawai'i as an exotic, and alluring Island. However, most of these images were fantasy, and lead to stereotyping that still exists to this day. Traditional Hawaiian women never wore grass skirts or coconut bras. The term *Hapa haole* means "half Caucasian," as in a description of a person who is defined as being of mixed Hawaiian and Caucasian ancestry. This usage stems from the fact that the first *haole* (non-Hawaiian) people encountered by the Hawaiians were Caucasians of northern European stock—with the exception of Caucasions of Portuguese ethnicity, who, by local custom and tradition are not considered to be *haole*. However, technically, all non-Hawaiians are *haole*.[10] *Hapa haole* music usually has English lyrics with a smattering of Hawaiian words. These songs first started becoming popular in the early 1900s, when practice of the Hawaiian language was suppressed. *Hapa haole* music was adapted over the years to match whatever musical style was popular at the time, ranging from ragtime, blues, and swing tunes. The *hapa haole* genre struck Broadway in 1912 in a play with music composed by David Evans, and lyrics by Winnie Holzman, called "Bird of Paradise." Shortly thereafter, the entire country was hooked, and listening to *hapa haole* tunes. Some Tin Pan Alley songwriters even went so far as to compose *hapa haole* songs that included made-up "Hawaiian" words. Composers centered in Hawai'i drew on their adoration of the Islands to construct songs of enduring beauty; songs like "My Fair Hawai'i," "Waikiki," and "Lovely Hula Hands" that were featured in Waikiki ballrooms, and on the well-known radio program of the day, "Hawai'i Calls." Following the Hawaiian Renaissance of the 1970s, that brought the Hawaiian language back to life, many regarded *hapa haole* music as inauthentic, and an apparatus of the tourism industry. However, the *hapa haole* genre has recently underwent its own rebirth and today is acknowledged for helping Hawai'i's music and composers to prosper even when the language seemed to be abandoned.

Mrs. Kaukini & Ms. Martha K. Maui

The names of these two women come down to us from Sonny Cunha's songbooks, "Songs of Hawai'i," (1902) and "Famous Hawaiian Songs" (1914). He lists the composer of "Hali'a-lau-lau" as that of Mrs. Kaukini, and the composer of "Ke Aloha Poina Ole" as being by Miss Martha K. Maui. Not much is known of these two women. However, these two songs utilize the same words, and very similar song structure as the song "Hi'ilawe" which is thought to be composed by Sam Li'a Kalainaina. Both songs follow a similar structure, both melodically and harmonically.

---

[10] Kanahele, George S., and John Berger. 2012. Hawaiian Music and Musicians: An Encyclopedic History. 1st ed. Hononlulu, HI: Mutual Publishing, LLC.
Page - 244

Thomas Sylvester Kalama

Thomas S. Kalama (1856-1906) published under the names Sylvester Kalama and Sylvester Thomas Kalama. He was the composer of several popular songs such as, "Maui Girl," "Wehiwehi Oe," "Kaleleonālani (Flight of the Royal Ones)," "One, Two, Three, Four," and "Pua Mikinolia." Kalama was inducted into the Hawaiian Music Hall of Fame in 2009. His granddaughter, Vicki I'i Rodrigues, was a well-respected musician, and authority of Hawaiian Music. She kept a notebook with several of her grandfather's compositions in it. Kalama composed *hapa haole* songs, as well as traditional Hawaiian arrangements, and originals.

Matthew Ho'onanai Kane

Matthew H. Kane (1872-1920) was born in Halawa, Molokai, Hawai'i. He was one of a number of Hawaiian singers who attended the mid-winter fair at San Francisco in 1894, and was a composer of several popular Hawaiian songs. He graduated from the Kamehameha school in 1893, and delivered the valedictory. He was also the principal at the Napoopoo government school. He was inducted into the Hawaiian Music Hall of Fame in 2013. Kane's compositions include "Ka Makani Ka'ilialoha," "Molokai Nui a Hina" and "'Aina Kaulana," better known as "Molokai Waltz." He co-wrote "Pua Carnation" with his Kamehameha School's classmate, Charles King.

James Fulton Kutz

James F. Kutz (1880-1976) was born in Mare Island, California. He attended the University of California, Berkeley, Class of 1904, and was a member of Delta Tau Delta fraternity. He was commissioned in the U.S. Navy, 1903, and served 43 years in the supply corps. He was Paymaster Pacific Fleet, stationed at Mare Island, California, during World War II. He was also a composer of songs including "Fair Hawai'i" recorded by Alfred Apaka and others.

Albert "Sonny" R. Cunha

Sonny Cunha (1879-1933) was a multitalented composer, arranger, pianist, vocalist, orchestra leader, businessman, and politician. He was educated at Saint Louis School and Punahou School and later attended Yale Law School in 1898, where he was a baseball and football star, although he did not graduate. He left behind an important legacy to Hawaiian music as the foremost promoter, and marketer of *hapa haole* songs. He was a major influence on Henry Kailimai and Johnny Noble, both of whom followed his precedent to institute the *hapa haole* song genre as an integral part of Hawaiian music. Cunha composed his first *hapa haole* song, "My Waikiki Mermaid," in 1903. His songs set the precedent for the genre as a whole. His book, *Famous Hawaiian Songs*, was the first book to include several *hapa haole* songs. He was also an active performer, performing his songs in Hawai'i and on the mainland. He toured the mainland for two years with his group and led his dance orchestra in Honolulu for many more.[11]

John "Johnny" Avery Noble

John Avery Noble (1892-1944) better known as Johnny Noble, was a musician, composer, and arranger. He was born in Honolulu, Hawai'i. He attended Kaiulani School, and in his spare time he sold newspapers on the streets of Honolulu and entertained passers-by whistling popular tunes. He attended High School at Saint Louis School, where he learned to play drums, piano and guitar. He graduated from school in 1911 and went to work at the Mutual Telephone Company in Honolulu, where he continued working long after he became a successful musician. Noble was a chief exponent in developing the *hapa haole* genre. Noble believed that jazz would blend perfectly with Hawaiian music. He put his theory to the test when he took over the Moano Orchestra. He used jazz harmonies, and rhythms in his arrangements. This gave the music a new lilting, syncopated swing. His new orchestra drew the largest crowds in Honolulu. Like Cunha before him, noble continued to change the *hapa haole* genre. His songs were almost entirely in English. Up until that point, *hapa haole* songs included at least a few English words to that of mostly Hawaiian. Noble reversed the trend, and his songs were mostly in English, with a few words of Hawaiian. Some have criticized Noble for "haolefying" Hawaiian music and imply that he was un-Hawaiian. However, he also composed many traditional Hawaiian hulas. Twenty-five are included in his collection *Hawaiian Hulas* which he published in 1934. Noble also played an important role in popularizing Hawaiian music via radio, publishing and performing. Moreover, in 1928, he directed the recording of 110 Hawaiian songs in Honolulu with recording equipment and a crew from the mainland.[12]

---

[11] Kanahele, George S., and John Berger. 2012. Hawaiian Music and Musicians: An Encyclopedic History. 1st ed. Hononlulu, HI: Mutual Publishing, LLC.
pages 115-116

[12] Kanahele, George S., and John Berger. 2012. Hawaiian Music and Musicians: An Encyclopedic History. 1st ed. Hononlulu, HI: Mutual Publishing, LLC.
pages 607-608.

John Milton "Jack" Owens

John Milton "Jack" Owens [13] (1912-1982) born in Tulsa, Oklahoma, was a singer/songwriter, pianist, and a star of the longest running network radio show, "Don McNeil's Breakfast Club." He was known as "The Cruising Crooner" because of his distinctive showmanship of strolling through mostly female audiences attending the live "Breakfast Club" broadcasts, and crooning love ballads to women, often singing directly to them, one at a time, sometimes even sitting on their laps. He started out his career with the job of holding the applause sign in local Chicago radio stations. He also performed briefly on the vaudeville circuit. From his fame on NBC and ABC as a radio singing star with movie star looks, Jack Owens found ways to stay in the spotlight in popular music with catchy songs, love ballads, and Hawaiian songs (*hapa haole*). Some of his music also appeared in such movies as *San Antonio Rose* in 1941 and *From Here to Eternity* in 1953. Jack Owens, who was married to fellow Chicago radio star Helen Streiff in the early 1930s, started his recording career with independent label, Tower Records. Soon after the huge success of "The Hukilau Song" and "I'll Weave a Lei of Stars for You" in 1948, he was signed to Decca, the largest label at the time. Disregarded or forgotten by many today, Owens was America's 10th favorite male vocalist from 1936 to 1944. He was best known for writing or co-writing such successful tunes as "Hi, Neighbor," "How Soon," "The Hukilau Song," and "I'll Weave a Lei of Stars for You." He either wrote, co-wrote, composed, or recorded more than 50 songs spanning from the mid-1930's to the early 1960's. He also had his own TV show, The Jack Owens Show during the pioneer days of TV of the early 1950s and even received two Emmy nominations.

Ukulele Stroke/Strum Techniques

When I arranged these pieces, I purposely left indications of what strokes to use out of the scores. I will leave it to the player to decide what strokes, or strums they want to utilize. There are no wrong strokes. In fact, one can use no strokes at all, and play the pieces all fingerstyle, and the arrangements will still work. This music has a certain improvisatory feel to it and lends itself to many possibilities. Use your imagination, and really make the pieces yours. However, I will include instructions for all of the various strokes that are possible. Also, I will include any strokes indicated by Bailey, or Awai for their arrangements. Furthermore, I will include the instructions for stroke techniques from Bailey's, and Awai's book: *The Ukulele as a Solo Instrument: A Collection of Ukulele Solos*. Bailey states in his book:

> After you have mastered using the Common Stroke, it will be both beneficial and interesting to experiment with various strokes. Endeavor to use those strokes which are most suitable to the rhythm and meaning of the composition. As previously stated, there are almost unlimited applications and combinations of strokes. The choice of strokes must be governed entirely by the performer.

---

[13] Picture loaned from the collection of Margaret Sanders.

THE COMMON STROKE

There are almost as many different applications of the stroke as there are players, but the Common Stroke as explained below is the foundation of it all. Once it is mastered thoroughly the rest will follow with comparative ease. The Common Stroke is made by swinging the end of the forefinger of the right hand lightly down and up across all the strings. Make the down stroke with the end of the nail (not the side) and the up stroke with the ball of the fleshy part of the finger. Keep the wrist high so that when the hand is in a perfectly relaxed condition the tip of the finger just touches the strings. The finger should brush the strings at about the upper part of the body of the Ukulele, this brings the wrist directly above the sound hole. Keep the wrist almost stationary and swing, or dangle, the hand back and forth by twisting the forearm. Avoid jerkiness.

THE ROLL STROKE

DOWN

Position of the hand same as in the Common Stroke. Strike, or drag, all the fingers down across all of the strings, holding the fingers about one inch apart, striking g first with the little finger, the other fingers following in their order in one continuous motion. This stroke is made obliquely by slightly lowering the wrist. When properly executed this produces a continuous rolling effect during the length of the stroke which is made in a deliberate manner. Sometimes the roll can be produced more effectively by starting with the third finger and in many cases, especially where a long slow roll is desired, the thumb can also be used at the finish of the stroke. The down roll stroke is used a great deal and should be practiced assiduously.

UP

This is a reversal of the Roll Stroke down. Bring the fingertips up across the strings, commencing with the thumb or forefinger. As the up stroke is nearly always more effective when the Common Stroke is used, (first finger only, or the thumb followed by the first finger only) too much time should not be devoted to the Roll Stroke up.

SYNCOPATED (Ragtime) STROKE

Example

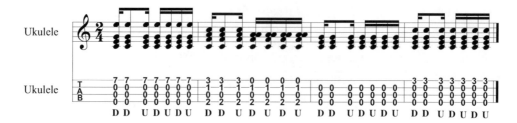

D – signifies a down stroke
U – signifies an up stroke
First Chord – use short, sharp, down stroke. It is not necessary to strike across all of the strings.
Second Chord – Slower down stroke. Emphasize this.
Third Chord – Short up stroke etc.
The rag stroke while it requires considerable practice is not difficult.
Remember – the hand and wrist must be perfectly flexible. Do not try to play loud. The fingers should merely brush the strings. In no other way can the Ukulele be played with true Hawaiian effect.

COMPOUND OR TRIPLE ROLL

The Triple Roll is a combination of two down strokes and one up stroke, as shown in the following exercise and when perfected, produces a continuous rolling effect. It is difficult and much practice will be necessary, but when thoroughly mastered will prove effective in all kinds of music.

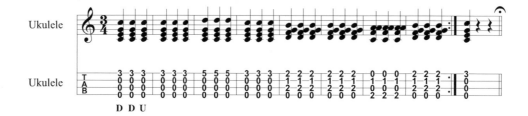

1st Chord – Down with forefinger as in Common Stroke.
2nd Chord – Down with ball of thumb.
3rd Chord – Up with ball of forefinger.

Practice very slowly, repeating many times, until the motion becomes automatic.
Keep the strokes even and the time steady.
Gradually increase the speed, but do not hurry.
Keep the thumb and forefinger about two inches apart.
Eventually the two down strokes will be made with one motion of the wrist.
In many cases the ordinary roll stroke down can be used as the stroke.
This however should be at the beginning of a roll as the effect
will not be clean and even, if used continuously.

TREMOLO STROKE

This is simply the common stroke (down & up) played rapidly, producing a tremolo effect.

EXAMPLE

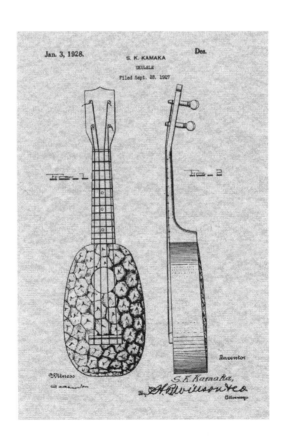

(Patent for Kamaka's Pineapple Ukulele Design)

Mauna Kea

Sonny Cunha
Arr. by George E. Awai

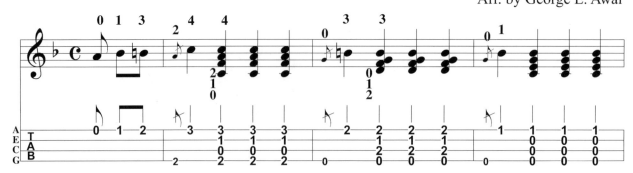
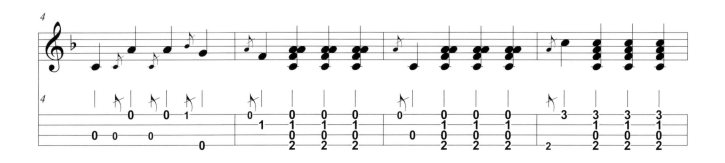
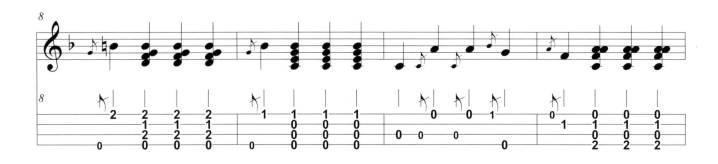
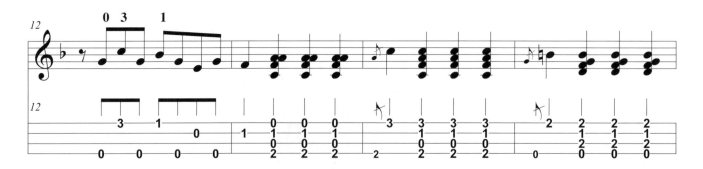

© Copyright by Gary Stewart, All Rights Reserved, International Copyright Secured, 2019

Mauna Kea

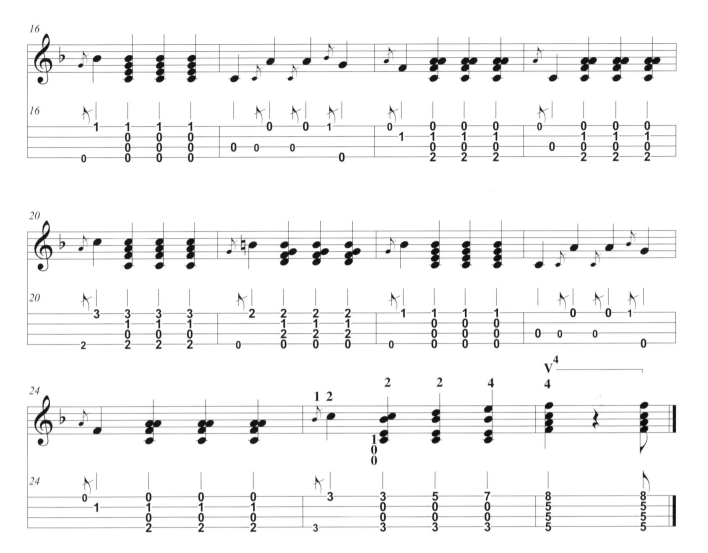

(Postcard published by Wall, Nichols & Co., ltd., Honolulu, 1910)

To Brittany Stewart

Roselani

W. J. Coelho
Arr. by Gary Stewart

© Copyright, 1916, by Charles E. King,
All Rights Reserved, International Copyright Secured, Gary Stewart, 2019

Roselani

Roselani

(Postcard #188 published by Hawai'i & South Seas Curio Co., Honolulu, 1920.)

The Hawaiian canoes are hollowed out of a single tree having strips of hardwood sewed on the upper edge of the canoe on each side, closing over the top at both stem and stern. The canoes are steadied by an out-rigger or Ama, a slender log of light wood parallel to the canoe and fastened to it by curve cross pieces or Iako.

To Stanley Yates
Song Of Old Hawai'i

Gordon Beecher & Johnny Noble
Arr. by Ernest K. Ka'ai

© Copyright by Gary Stewart, All Rights Reserved, International Copyright Secured, 2019

Song Of Old Hawai'i

Maui Girl

27

Maui Girl

Maui Girl

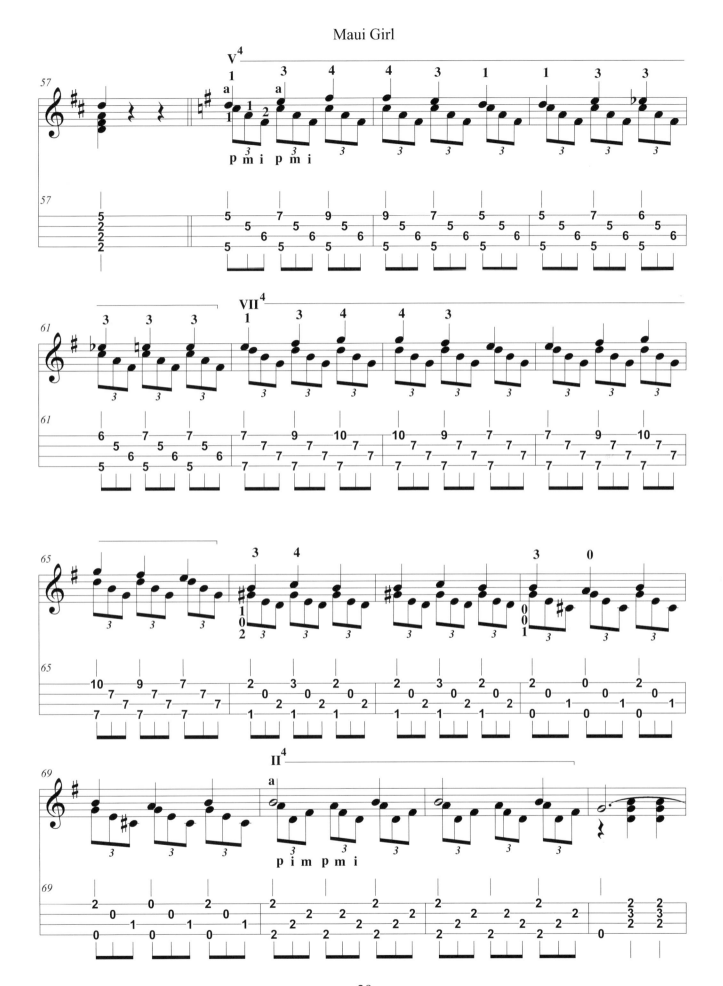

Maui Girl

Maui Girl

Maui Girl

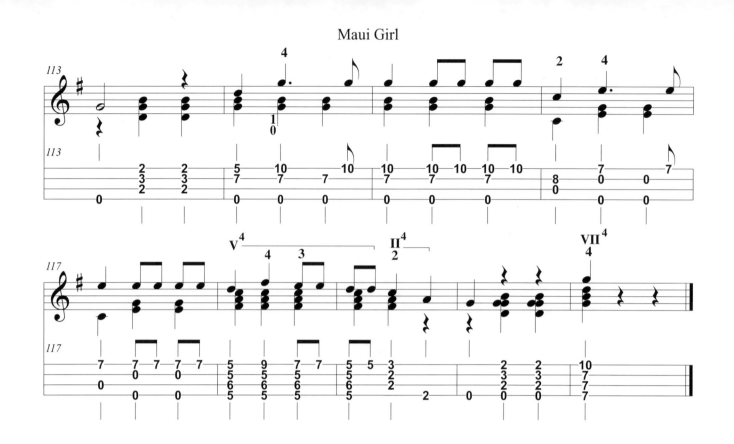

(Hawaiian Girl, published by Honolulu Paper Co., 1917)

To Lelaloha
Kuu Iini
(My Desire)

Charles E. King
Arr. Gary Stewart

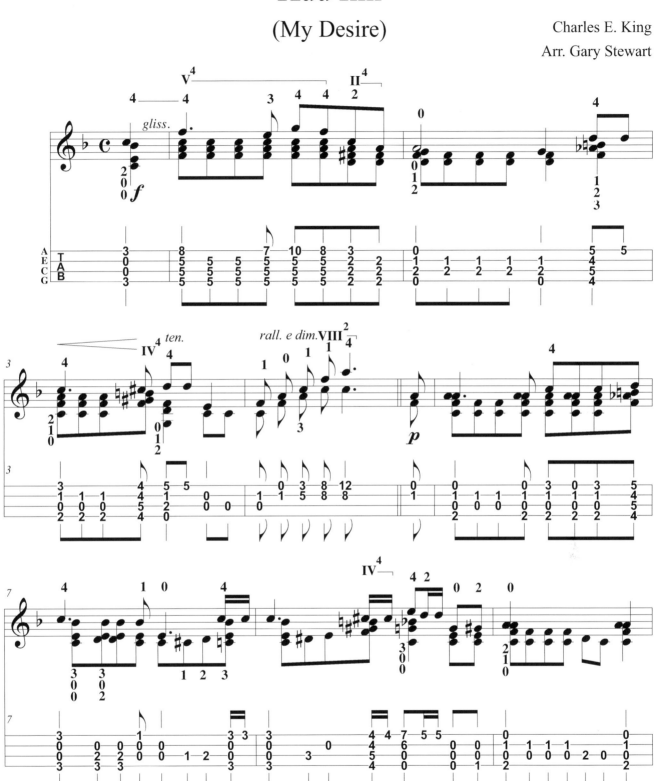

Kuu Iini

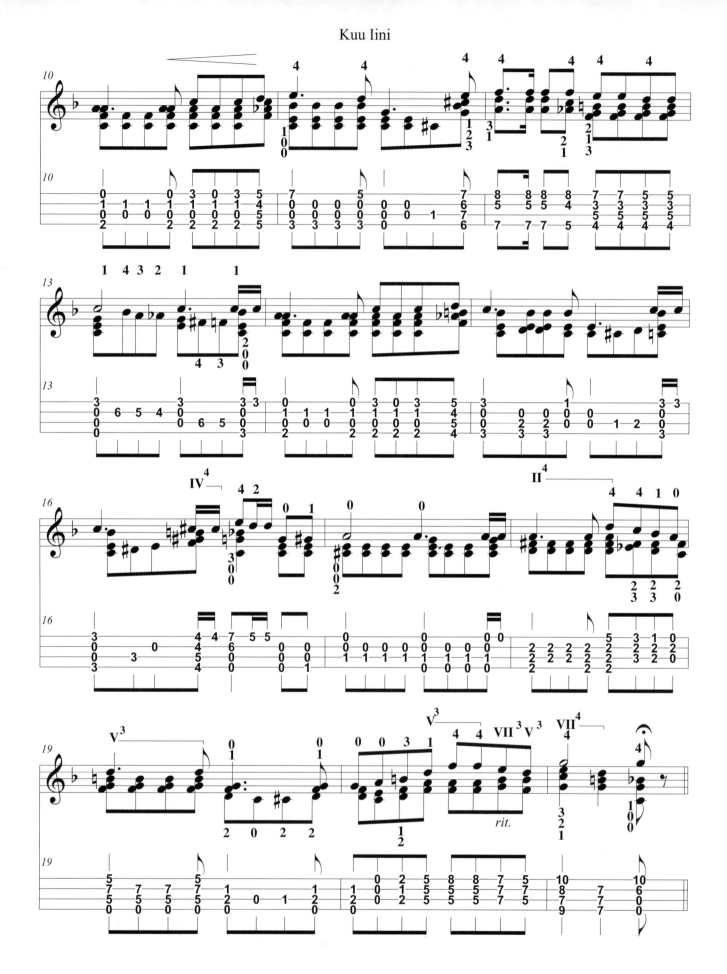

Kuu Iini

35

To Rebbecca N. Barnes

My Dear Hawai'i

Charles E. King
Arr. by Gary Stewart

My Dear Hawai'i

View of Diamond Head from Kapiolani Park.
(Postcard published by Hawaiian Curio Co., Honolulu, 1910)

Diamond Head is a volcanic tuff cone on the Hawaiian island of Oʻahu and known to Hawaiians as Lēʻahi. Its English name was given by British sailors in the 19th century, who mistook calcite crystals on the adjacent beach for diamonds.[1]

Clark, John R. K. *Hawai'i Place Names: Shores, Beaches, and Surf Sites*. University of Hawaii Press, Honolulu, 2002. pp. 60.

To Easton Barnes

On the Beach At Waikiki

Henry Kailimai

Arr. by George E. Awai

(1892 photograph by J.J. Williams)
A Hawaiian surfer at Waikiki Beach, carrying a traditional Alalia (surf) board.

© Copyright by Gary Stewart, All Rights Reserved, International Copyright Secured, 2019

To Cynthia Turner

Sweet Brown Maid of Kaimuki

Henry Kailimai
Arr. by George E. Awai

© Copyright by Gary Stewart, All Rights Reserved, International Copyright Secured, 2019

Sweet Brown Maid of Kaimuki

Ka Makani Ka'ili Aloha

Halialaulani / Ke Aloha Poina Ole

Mrs. Kaukini and Miss Martha K. Maui
Arr. by Gary Stewart

Tempo di Hula

© Copyright 1902 by William H. Coney, Honolulu, T.H.,
All Rights Reserved, International Copyright Secured, Gary Stewart, 2019

Halialaulani / Ke Aloha Poina Ole

45

Halialaulani / Ke Aloha Poina Ole

Halialaulani / Ke Aloha Poina Ole

Halialaulani / Ke Aloha Poina Ole

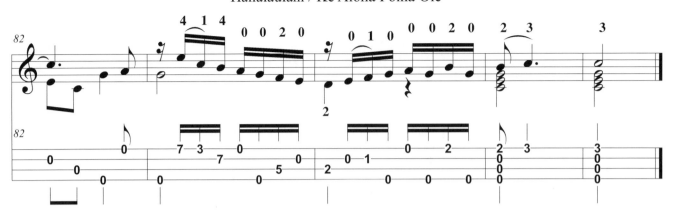

(Hawaiians Dancing the Hula)
Illustration from: Badan Whettran, Pearls of the Pacific, 1876

(Postcard published by Moses Stationery Co., Milo, Hawai'i, 1920)

This was a typical cane flume that was constructed throughout Hawai'i for transporting the sugar from the Highlands direct to the mill. After 180 years of sugar production on the islands, Hawaii's last remaining sugar plantation closed in 2016.

To Yvonne Stewart

Fair Hawai'i

James Fulton Kutz
Arr. by N. B. Bailey

Fair Hawai'i

(Original cover from "Fair Hawai'i," Sherman, Clay & Co., 1914)

To Kamehamehame School

Kamehameha Waltz

Charles E. King
Arr. by Gary Stewart

© Copyright by Charles E. King, 1917,
All Rights Reserved, International Copyright Secured, Gary Stewart, 2019

Kamehameha Waltz

Kamehameha Waltz

(Postcard published by Mid-Pacific Curio Store, Honolulu 1917)
The Bernice Pauahi Bishop Museum located on the Kamehameha School Grounds.

To Kuliaikanuu Colburn

Paauau Waltz

Charles E. King
Arr. by Gary Stewart

Valse Moderato

© Copyright, 1916, by Charles E. King,
All Rights Reserved, International Copyright Secured, Gary Stewart, 2019

Paauau Waltz

Paauau Waltz

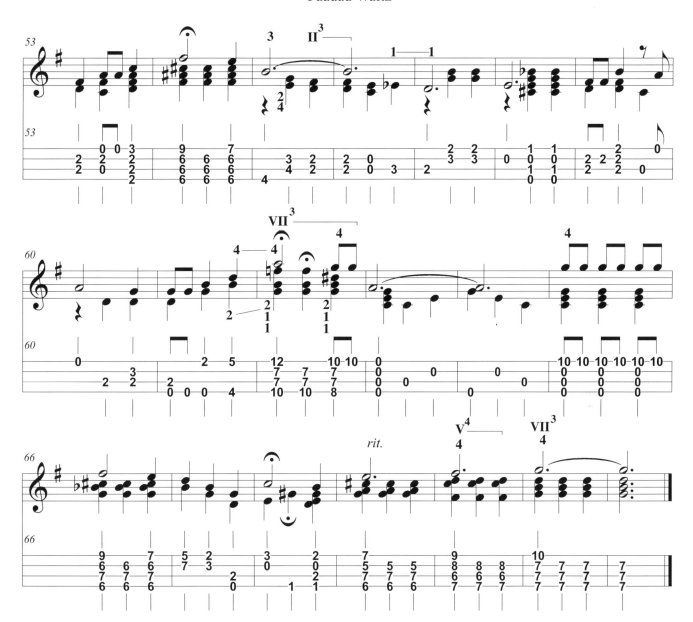

Manuel Nunes emigrated to Hawaii from Madeira in 1879, and became a key player in the transformation of the Madeiran machete, into the Hawaiian ukulele. He was one of the first ukulele makers, and operated his manufacturing company for over 40 years. Most of his instruments were inscribed with the label, "M. Nunes, Inventor of the Ukulele and Taro Patch Fiddles in Honolulu in 1879." He passed on his trade to apprentices such as Samuel Kamaka, and his son Leonardo Nunes, both of whom carried on the tradition of crafting fine handmade ukuleles.

Dedicated to Hon. John F. Colburn

Paauau Hula

Charles E. King
Arr. by Gary Stewart

Paauau Hula

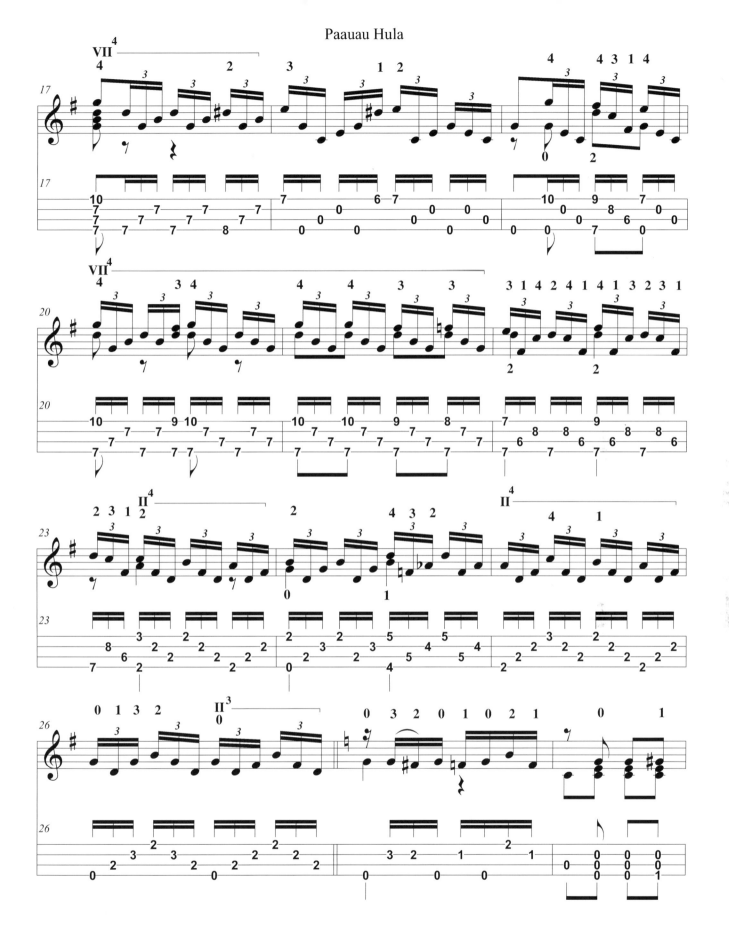

Paauau Hula

Paauau Hula

(Postcard publishes by Hawai'i South Seas Curio Co., Honolulu, 1918)

To Jimmy "Junior" Marston

The Hukilau Song

Jack Owens
Arr. by Gary Stewart

©Copyright, 1948, Owens-Kemp Music Co.,
All Rights Reserved, International Copyright Secured, Gary Stewart, 2019

The Hukilau Song

The Hukilau Song

(Postcard published by Hawai'i & South Seas Co., Honolulu, 1921)

(Postcard published by Honolulu Paper Co., Honolulu, 1919)

The native grass houses, formerly in great abundance, have now been displaced by frame houses. They were, in many instances, built with considerable regard to appearance and were particularly suitable to the balmy climate of Hawai'i. The illustration shows native Hawaiians making poi in front of a grass house.

To Mark Barnes

Pauoa Liko Lehua

(Pauoa, Home of the Lehua)

Charles E. King
Arr. by Gary Stewart

© Copyright, 1924, by Charles E. King,
All Rights Reserved, International Copyright Secured, Gary Stewart 2019

Pauoa Liko Lehua

Elue Mikimiki

(Postcard published by Mid-Pacific Curio Store, Honolulu, 1923)

The Hula Blues

To Gary W. Stewart Sr.

John Avery Noble
Arr. by Gary Stewart

The Hula Blues

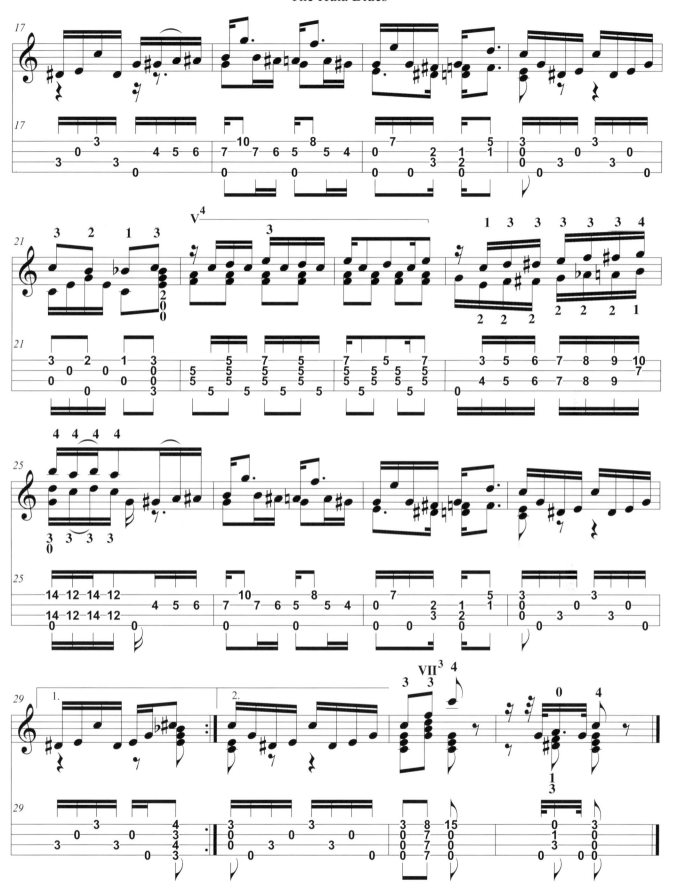

71

To Harley A. Scott

My Honolulu Hula Girl

Sonny Cunha
Arr. by N. B. Bailey

© Copyright by the Bergstrom Music Co., 1909,
All Rights Reserved, International Copyright Secured, Gary Stewart, 2019

My Honolulu Hula Girl

Postcard published by Hawaiian Curio Co., Honolulu, 1924

To Lillian Barnes
Aloha O'e
(Farewell to Thee)

Lydia Lili'uokalani
Arr. by George E. Awai

Aloha O'e

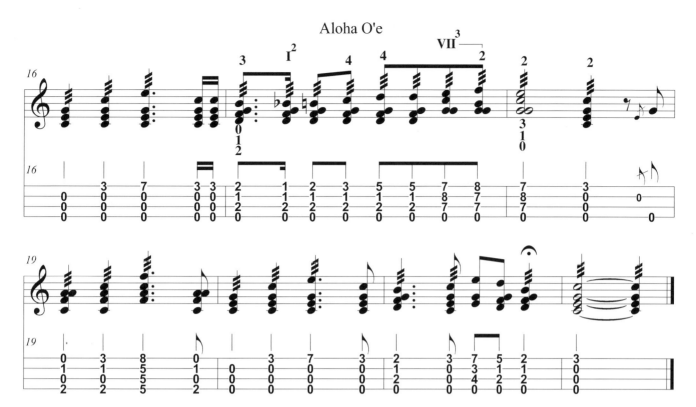

(Cover of sheet music published by Sherman, Clay & Co., 1909)

About the Author

Gary Stewart

A native of Kentucky, Gary Stewart began playing the piano, banjo, ukulele, and viola as a child. Stewart has performed as a soloist, chamber musician, and lecturer for several festivals and concert series. He was a top prize-winning guitarist in several guitar competitions such as, The Rantucci International Guitar Competition (New York), The Southeastern Guitar Congress Guitar Competition (Alabama), The Young Persons Beethoven Club Competition (Tennessee), and the Jim Stroud Guitar Competition (Ohio). Stewart has also been the recipient of several composition dedications. Stewart has also world premiered several guitar concerti, and chamber works with various orchestras, and chamber ensembles. Stewart has performed and recorded with The Cleveland Baroque Orchestra and the Cleveland Opera. His recording with Apollo's Fire on Avie records, entitled *Come to the River*, was released internationally and debuted in the Classical Billboard top 10. He has also recorded over 150 pieces for the Guitar Foundation of America archive. He completed his undergraduate studies in guitar performance with Dr. Stanley Yates at Austin Peay State University, his master's degree studies with Stephon Aron (Oberlin Conservatory) at Akron University, and concluded his doctoral studies with Dr. Glenn Caluda at Shenandoah Conservatory.

(Cover of Aloha O'e, published by W.A. Quincke & Co., California, ca. 1912)

Made in the USA
Coppell, TX
27 April 2024

31768503R00044